SIX-WORD
MEMOIRS
ON LOVE
&
HEARTBREAK

Also from SMITH Magazine

Not Quite What I Was Planning:
Six-Word Memoirs by Writers Famous & Obscure

SIX-WORD
MEMOIRS
ON LOVE
&
HEARTBREAK

by Writers Famous & Obscure

From SMITH *Magazine*

Edited by
Rachel Fershleiser *and*
Larry Smith

HARPER  PERENNIAL

NEW YORK • LONDON • TORONTO • SYDNEY • NEW DELHI • AUCKLAND

HARPER  PERENNIAL

The editors would like to thank SMITH Magazine cofounder Tim Barkow; our agent, Kate Lee; our editor, Kate Hamill; and the whole crew at Harper Perennial.

We are eternally appreciative of the many bloggers who spread the word about *Six-Word Memoirs on Love & Heartbreak* and SMITH's other projects. Most of all, we're grateful for and inspired by the thousands of memoirists who share their stories, six words at a time, each and every day.

Share your six-word memoir on love or another topic at sixwordmemoirs.com. Share any true story at SMITH Magazine, smithmag.net.

HarperCollins books may be purchased for educational, business, or sales promotional use. For information please write: Special Markets Department, HarperCollins Publishers, 10 East 53rd Street, New York, NY 10022.

FIRST EDITION

Designed by Justin Dodd

Library of Congress Cataloging-in-Publication Data is available upon request.

ISBN 978-0-06-171462-7

09 10 11 12 13   OV/RRD   10 9 8 7 6 5 4 3 2 1

Introduction

We launched SMITH Magazine (www.SMITHmag
.net) in 2006 because we've always believed in the power
of storytelling. Collecting six-word memoirs, as we've
been doing for more than two years now, has taught us
even more than we imagined. When Ernest Heming-
way famously wrote "For Sale: baby shoes, never worn,"
he proved that an entire story can be told using a half
dozen words. When we first asked readers to submit
six-word memoirs back in December 2006, we realized
a whole, real life can be conveyed this way, too. We've
learned about honesty and bravery and good writing,

often from people who hadn't considered themselves "writers." We've witnessed how generous people can be in sharing their stories, and how much it means to them to be asked.

People around the world told us of happiness and pain ("Found true love, married someone else"), success and failure ("Never really finished anything, except cake"), and how rarely the path we start on is the one we take to the completion of a journey ("After Harvard, had baby with crackhead"). Perhaps contributor Summer Grimes really did say it best—for most of us, life is "not quite what I was planning." We used her memoir as the title of our first book, and it was a hit, even making the *New York Times* bestseller list—for *six* weeks, as luck would have it.

The most exciting thing about the success of *Not Quite What I Was Planning: Six-Word Memoirs by Writers Famous & Obscure* has been watching other people re-imagine the form. From kindergarten through graduate school, teachers brought the six-word storytelling exercise into their classrooms. A reverend in North Carolina preached six-word prayers to his congregation, and a young girl in California ended her eulogy for her poker-loving grandma with a six-word summation of her life ("Look, I have a royal flush!"). An exercise instructor used these mini-memoirs to keep his cycling students pumping, and an Alzheimer's sufferer turned to our stories when longer ones proved too challenging to remember. A composer decided to begin a six-word song cycle, and after a blogger challenged her readers to write a six-word memoir and then "tag" five friends, a six-word memoir "meme" began racing across hundreds of thousands of personal blogs all over the world. It continues to grow as we write these words.

Six-word memoirs still pour into SMITH every day. As we've sifted through piles of briefly encapsulated lives, we've seen themes emerge, from faith to hair to masturbation to French fries. By far the most common thread, however, is love. Passionate love, parental love, platonic love—it seemed to be the most universally life-changing factor for storytellers of every age, background, and worldview.

This book celebrates life in all its shades of red—a valentine, if you will, to every kind of love. But it's also a nod to love's evil twin: heartache. So many of our favorite memoirs, from "Ex-wife and contractor now have house" to "Girlfriend is pregnant, my husband said," reflect the other side of Cupid's coin—the breakups and losses that make the hard-won magical moments that much more powerful.

We've once again brought you a book that's a grab bag of the famous and unknown. Both types of memoirist are inspiring, and often it won't matter which you're reading. You don't have to be a fashionista to feel each and every one of designer Marc Ecko's six words: "It never hurt as good again." If you've read Elizabeth Gilbert's book *Eat, Pray, Love*, then her six words, "My life's accomplishments? Sanity, and you," carry extra-special meaning. If you haven't, you still appreciate the sentiment.

The oft-quoted Tolstoy line "All happy families are alike; each unhappy family is unhappy in its own way" seems to hold true for relationships as well. It was frequently the six-word stories of complications or even misery that we found most fascinating and deeply felt. Entire books lie beneath "Teen homewrecker. Still miss his kid," "She got Hodgkin's lymphoma. I bailed," and "War destroyed his heart and mine."

Of course the happily-ever-afters have their own charm, and some of the most touching stories come from those who've found the secret of everlasting love. Late Yankees great Bobby Murcer and his wife, Kay, offer a pair of memoirs on page 21. They met when he was eleven, she nine. "When Kay flashed those big brown eyes my way, I was a goner!" he told us just months before he passed away. "Been gazing into them for over fifty years!" Kay said, "We have opposing personality traits, but our daily dose of laughter is the key to marital bliss."

We also mined love stories from some more mismatched contributors. We've got memoirists gay, straight, single, married, divorced, and polyamorous, hailing from Australia to Vietnam. An entry by sex columnist Dan Savage sits alongside one by Pulitzer Prize–winning poet Robert Hass. Janice Dickinson dishes out six words of advice in the brazen spirit she's known for, while Chip Rowe—a.k.a. The Playboy Advisor—reveals something we suspect he's never told his millions of readers. And what has the world's most famous divorce lawyer, Raoul Felder, learned about love? Heartbreaking, indeed.

We hope this book will provide some laughs, some glimmers of recognition, and some moments of solace. Under the covers with your sweetheart, over cocktails with friends, or alone with a tube of cookie dough, you'll find real life on every page. Ponder the stories, write your own, and tell them at sixwordmemoirs.com.

Lastly, we offer this six-word suggestion: Share them with someone you love.

The Editors of SMITH Magazine
January 2009
New York, NY

SIX-WORD
MEMOIRS
ON LOVE
&
HEARTBREAK

Offered my heart; he embraced it.

—Sue Kimber

Should have read the pre-nup agreement.

—Loranne Brown

**Not always perfect.
But so worthwhile.**

—Lauren Anderson

Lost my virginity to her husband.

—Shawna Mayer

Red-eye. Him window.
Me aisle. Love.

—*Joanne Flynn Black*

Thought "great legs!"
Said "great smile!"

—*Lionel Ancelet*

Coffee, my vice. So was he.

—*Alessandra Rizzotti*

**If I get Chlamydia,
blame MySpace.**

—*Hanorah Slocum*

What once were two, are one.

—*George Saunders*

I never said "I love you."

—*S. Lynn Taylor*

Don't trust a man who waxes.

—*Noelle Hancock*

Waited for her to be legal.

—*Jonathan Lesser*

Lovesick. 1985. Suicide by Pop Rocks.

—*Jaynel Attolini*

She got back on the Vespa.

—Josh McHugh

Magnetic attraction
fused two polar opposites.

—Phil Sylvester

He's dumb but lifts
heavy stuff.

—Laura Fausset

Will government ever let us marry?

—Vicki Marsh

I think it was the cassoulet.

—*Amy Ephron*

Never forget, I love you madly.

—*Alan Rader*

Love blooms like crocuses:
  dirty, brave.

—Antay Bilgutay

  Feasted, fasted, festered, fostered.
Fisted? Ewww.

—Ben Karlin

I wasn't supposed to meet you.

—Deborah Greene

Silently suffered
his facial hair
experiments.

—Elizabeth Minkel

War destroyed his heart and mine.

—*Dr. Maggie McClure*

Met him online.
Blogged our divorce.

—*Kristy Sammis*

Erectile dysfunction doesn't
kill true love.

—*Karin Poklen*

No, you can't have the
toaster.

—*Diana Spechler*

Should have listened to
the soothsayer.

—*Lisa Johnson*

While playing
wingman, found
my wife.

—*Scott Northrup*

Ten-year romance without
your participation.

—*Amanda Pawesk*

Parents:
"Mentioning homosexuality
upsets your brother."

—*Dean Morris*

Seeking Hell, finding Heaven.
Very disappointed.

—*Richard Zacks*

He left his wife
for me.

—*Selina Fire*

Westernized

Indian

+

Sassy American

=

Doomed Pair

—*Nancy Salerno*

Tongue in her mouth. She gagged.

—*R. F. Marazas*

A kiss can write a secret.

—Annmarie Howell

**He posted our
sex tape online.**

—Lauran Strait

`It never hurt as
good again.`

—Marc Ecko

He makes me laugh
every day.

—Detta Owens

Massage parlor breeds heir
of adultery.

—*Lorri Scott*

Unrequited love is just
another addiction.

—*Amanda Faith Moore*

Found Jewish princess.
Good-bye succulent pork.

—*Leah Damski*

Love. Loss. Love lost.
Stories gained.

—*Kristen Jones*

You wouldn't litter,
but cheated plenty.

—*Jennifer I. Curtis*

Sleeping, our foreheads touch.
Fates mingle.

—*Sandhya Nankani*

Wanted a wife. Got a cat.

—*Anders Porter*

My mother warned
me about you.

—*Angie Brown*

Teenage kiss. Misadventures.
Five-day date. Matrimony.

—*Julie Oppenheimer*

Married for sex;
divorced for politics.

—*Maryanne Stahl*

Neglect induced fatal
    condition. Heart
    amputated.

—*Pat Wahler*

I just wasn't that into him.

—*Mia Lipsit*

Got the ring. Mailed it back.

—Cindy Box

My hypothalamus
washed my wallet
clean.

—Dan Pulcrano

Now married, kissing with eyes open.

—Elissa Schappell

I thought I had thick skin.

—Tanja Cilia

Boyfriend? In the
nightstand with
batteries.

—*David James*

He liked vodka more than me.

—*Lauren Mitchell*

Three marriages.
Two divorces.
BA .333.

—*Ron Carmean*

Leg man trapped inside
breast man.

—*Fjord Fellraps*

Maybe some pots have no lids.

—*Melissa Gould*

**Seven days turned
into forty-six years.**

—*Harriette Spanabel*

Drive-in movie was better
than date.

—*Gail B. Burk*

Lucky me. I found the one.

—*Ellie Keen*

He died. I lived. You came.

—*Judi Kolenda*

Found myself a nerdy
computer programmer.

—*Jennifer 8. Lee*

Manhattan presents countless
options. It's problematic.

—*John Godfrey*

Hearts never look both
ways first.

—*Tanya Jarrett*

Don't worry, I'll make myself come.

—*Amy Sohn*

Lazy mornings.
Sunday *Times*.
Then: kids.

—*Marisa de los Santos*

I loved the idea of you.

—*Audrey Adu-Appiah*

Alone by chance,
not by choice.

—*Catherine Lanser*

I couldn't get on the plane.

—*Darcy Totten*

Her beautiful eyes . . .
my guiding light!

—*Bobby Murcer*

He's velcro, I'm teflon . . .
Love endures!

—*Kay Murcer*

He asked me to abort.
Dumbass.

—*Barbara Cromarty*

Became the other woman.
Didn't know.

—*Cameron Vest*

Strange relationship:
we both wore dresses.

—*Dylan Fox*

When he left me, he cried.

—*Ella Cristina*

Jim slept here; so did Carlos.

—Gloria Palazzo

The one for me married him.

—Francis McEvoy

Waited out cancer;
you said bye.

—Joe Carlson

Found my ex-husband on Craigslist. Twice.

—Yin Shin

Car went kaput. So did he.

—*Lori Romero*

My partner in sin
found God.

—*Marie D'Avignon*

Moved in. No ring. Moved out.

—*Melissa Lafsky*

Will always follow you.
On Twitter.

—*Mircea Lungu*

I never said I wanted this.

—*Melchor Sahagun*

He wrote songs for me. Sigh.

—*Pamela Des Barres*

He impregnated her instead.
Bullet dodged.

—*Judith Edelman*

One diamond necklace later,
I'm single.

—*Michael Collins*

Singles ad, double wide, triple bypass.

—*Ray Overfield*

Left my bed to marry her.

—*LoraMarie Mitchell*

Last encounter:
    crowded nightclub.
        Ran away.

—*Tom Dolby*

He's off heroin and crack—
yay!

—*Tricia Boczkowski*

The medication made him feel numb.

—*Tori Turner*

She said she
liked my penis.

—*Chip Rowe*

Siren wooed.
Sailor swooned.
Man overboard!

—*Jim Ruland*

Stalked him until he
married me!

—*Tiffany Mesquite*

Soulmate found in grade nine gym.

—*Amy Leask*

You holding my hair, me puking.

—*Diana Greiner*

I'm not marrying for love twice.

—*Lisa Baron*

Reclaimed maiden name after every divorce.

—*Victoria Martin*

Married by Elvis, divorced by Friday.

—G. M. Rouse

For the children, I remain his.

—Gisele Phipps

May/December ... the
best of seasons.

—Julie Howe

Arranged marriage now
sounding pretty good.

—Saleem Reshamwala

First college sweethearts,
now happily married.

—Jason Pinter

This crazy dream
I lived died.

—*Julian Rubinstein*

**Around the world in
eighty guys.**

—*K. C. Sanders*

If it's limping,
shoot it dead.

—*Lesley Blum*


```
We belly laugh every
single day.
```

—*Michelle Ottey*

Where's the love? he asked, confused.

—*Jessica Yu*

Baseball is much better without you.

—*Nicole Phillips*

Smooches cause
bruises
but also
papooses.

—*David Nadelberg*

Once cute stubble,
now scraggly beard.

—*Debra Thurston*

Obsession with garlic unhelpful, I've learned.

—*Nathaniel Rich*

Happy enough . . . was her tentative reply.

—*Salli Hollenzer*

He's less tall but more sane.

—*Stephanie Losee*

They both hated wide ruled paper.

—*Scarborough Fairchild*

We met on Halloween. No costumes.

—*Dani Shapiro*

I thought we had more time.

—*Joe Hill*

Single by chance;
mother by choice.

—*Chanda Gunn*

```
SWM hemophiliac seeks
SWF knife thrower.
```

—*Allen Jones*

My life's accomplishments?
Sanity, and you.

—*Elizabeth Gilbert*

Cuddling in bed, she said
good-bye.

—*Christopher Warren*

People can't want what they
want.

—*Dr. Drew Pinsky*

And his relationship status
said "Married."

—*Genevieve Donaldson*

Only once. It was a doozy.

—*Marc Mondfrans*

Where he is, I am home.

—*Julia Evans*

Marriage is annual contract,
renew wisely.

—*Kristi James*

Surprise! Her affairs turn
husband on.

—*Laurie Simpkinson*


```
Bachelor visits
library, books wife
(nonfiction).
```

—*Michael Perry*

I always take love frivolously
serious.

—*Xaviera Hollander*

```
Portland, she
decided; I,
the Bronx.
```

—*Dominic Preziosi*

I trusted her forever.
Good choice.

—*Nate Koechley*

Internet exploitation at thirteen,
dating impaired.

—*Jessie Rippel*

Good sex was all we had.

—*Kimberley Yvette Price*

I write. He shoots.
We edit.

—*Claire Zulkey*

Fake agony over farts in bed.

—*Jim Gladstone*

Broken, livid, silent,
vomit. Still there.

—*Yael Levy*

Married the second
guy who asked.

—*Erin McQuade Kennedy*

My mother died.
You're not her.

—*Jonathan Marc Sherman*

His wife offered
herself too late.

—*A. T. Lynne*

Two people. Twelve years.
One divorce.

—*Amanda Joann Smith*

It's like my
heart has
sciatica.

—Jonathan Ames

Waiting to forget your name
again.

—*Cybele Paschke*

In the beginning,
I showered daily.

—*Deena Drewis*

No visas,
no addicts,
no crazies.

—*Rebecca Caddy*

Your planet: Peter. My planet: Earth.

—*Elinor McKay*

He is married. I am not.

—*Hope Truhart*

Horoscopes were
compatible: divorce court
ahead!

—*Georgia Hubley*

**The apartment is
much cleaner now.**

—*Daniel J. Stasiewski*

Loved. Lost.
Cried. Raged.
Chocolate.
Next.

—*Jackie Childress*

**Arrived with hope,
   left with heartache.**

—*Kacey Barron*

**Thank you for
breaking my heart.**

—*Mia Kirshner*

**Dumped me because
God said to.**

—*Lauren Gibaldi*

Forgot why I left;
went back.

—*Sharon Lewis*

Marry for love, again and again.

—Deborah Rodriguez

Not him again!
said my mother.

—Lisa Ihnken


```
I left town and
died, alone.
```

—Eric J. Millar

Mr. Wrong introduced
me to Right.

—Amy Fudally

She knows what my
Kryptonite is.

—Matt Ruff

46

His country house was painted black.

—*Robin Palme*

Lost a lover;
gained a lawyer.

—*Matt Mather*

Discovered my love is in Him.

—*Eboni Stewart*

It helps to label
the books.

—*Juan Antonio del Rosario*

Forced into being Jewish By Choice.

—*Mariah I. Garving*

**Romance remembered
often better than
experienced.**

—*Jean Feingold*

What do *you* want
for dinner?

—*Drew Magary*

Met girl, moved abroad,
she followed.

—*Cody Barkley*

He loved her more than me.

—Shelby Mulhare

Butterflies still kicking after
  ten years.

—Lisa Taylor

Found soul mate.
Became cell mate.

—Harlan Stanton

He preferred "fuck"
over "make love."

—Jessica Chalmers

But his sweat tasted like mushrooms.

—*Kathryn Kreimer*

He punched my car. The End.

—*Marya Hornbacher*

Love plus laughter: happily ever after.

—*Dan Goggin*

Tried many; selected the finest one.

—*Maria Nestorides*

Worried the dog liked him better.

—*Lindsay Ross*

Said "I do."
Screamed "I don't."

—*Shawn Lea*

Could not give up
the remote.

—*Doni Gewirtzman*

Good men? Like promises,
easily broken.

—*Bill West*

He still needs me

at sixty-four.

—*Armistead Maupin*

Her funeral made us a couple.

—*Allison Joseph*

My husband texted her,
"Wanna fuck?"

—*Elisha Boudreau*

If only he wasn't a Republican.

—*Holly Fitzpatrick*

**Visiting Belizean
prison, must be love.**

—*Jenny Kessler*

Proposed under windchimes,
gusty winds ahead.

—*Melissa Marlene Laurie*

Second time, for love and money.

—*Ronald Zalewski*

Said good-bye. Murdered
our future forever.

—*Twanna Hines*

Marriage coaching didn't work. I'm faking.

—*Laurie Schmidt*

**Lust walked in.
Love walked out.**

—*Amy Sedivy*

`Marry me, boy, said`
`the cougar.`

—*Kat Shehata*

Happy in convent.
Then grace left.

—*Amelia Perkins*

Remaining married despite
infidelity and in-laws.

—*H. D. Driggers*

```
He lied, cheated, left;
bestselling memoir.
```
—Laura Fraser

It's worth it, despite your mother.
—Samantha MacFarlane

In his smile I saw forever.
—Aliviah Sauers

Never thought I'd marry a
mortician.
—Meaghan O'Neill

Monogamists meet at sex party, marry.

—*Molly Ditmore*

Critical, clenched
husband. Heavy, heavy
heart.

—*Natalie Shrock*


```
Thought Yiddish.
Married British.
Oy! Oi!
```

—*Rachel Pine*

Preferred brunettes but
kept the blond.

—*Rebecca Stadolnik*

He liked me for my race.

—Tommy Wong

Still have hope. Maybe he'll change.

—Ariel Leve

Love, a rose. Velvet petals, thorny.

—Sharon Haymes

We married twice. We divorced twice.

—Veronica Honer

Love
almost
always
leads to
heartbreak.

—*Raoul Felder, Esq.*

I cleaned. He cleaned me out.

—Naomi Major

Love at first sight
is blind.

—Jace Albao

I came. He conquered.
We divided.

—Jen Kocher

I married three times too
many.

—Winnie Shrader

Tried men.
  Tried women.
Like cats.

—*Dona Bumgarner*

He cut his hair:
thrill gone.

—*Rosie Clarke*

She called. Friend answered.
  Lost both.

—*Ellis Reyes*

Overly romantic soul,
born wrong era.

—*Elisa Shevitz*

62

Found love at forty-six. Who knew?

—*Dixie Feldman*

Leap of faith.
Shit, no parachute.

—*Katherine Yunker*

6'3" guy in my Neon backseat.

—*Kelly Kovaleski*

You loved, lied, cheated, me too.

—*Kristin Knudsen*

At twelve found soulmate,
  still together.

—Nancy Miner

**Despise him. Desperately
seek his approval.**

—Beth Linas

`Inevitably, his`
`  obituary didn't`
`  mention me.`

—R. Sue Dodea

My heart is
  my strongest
muscle.

—Shanna Katz

Heartbroken, until
the bitch finally
died.

—*Christopher Moore*

Incest: Nothing was
ever the same.

—*Laura Davis*

Kissed
many frogs.
Finally found
prince.

—*Lacie Cannon*

Good as friends,
disaster as lovers.

—*Shani Friedman*

He told me he was single.

—Esther Newberg

Loved. Lost. Loved again. Worth it.

—Erika Jakubassa

He e-mailed again and I deleted.

—Molly Antopol

Love: eight pounds and six ounces.

—Kenny Clark

Walking away, never saw her face.

—*Robert MacLeod*

Right people. Wrong
time. Wrong place.

—*Tina Wells*

My tattoo,
his name,
our secret.

—*Susan Breeden*

I should have seen
him coming.

—*Kelly Bruce*

He always stirs my chocolate milk.

—*Sarah Thornburg*

Their divorce, his Viagra,
her insurance.

—*Kathy Service*

She wanted Gatsby.
Got "Gets By."

—*Beth Connellan*

Therapist:
"You went
back after
that?"

—*Neil Thornton*

Still can't believe
I kissed him.

—*Rosally Sapla*

Long distance didn't make
love easier.

—*Rachel Kramer Bussel*

My book title makes dating
awkward.

—*V. V. Ganeshananthan*

**Big ambitions. Chased
women. Oh well . . .**

—*Don Cummer*

`Child bride sticks
with first love.`

—*Erika Munson*

I asked, sadly she said no.

—*Judy Hasday*

We were roadkill on
love's highway.

—*Kyla E. Town*

It was always better
with strangers.

—*Igby Kin*

Replaced by a mail-order
bride.

—*Marissa Jacobe*

Screwed. Screwed Up.
Settled down. Happier.

—*Steve Almond*

Oh, I loved you so much . . .

—*Tillie Seger*

He was "our" dog—
not anymore.

—*Chris Teja*

Red flags all over China,
heartbroken.

—*Amy Blumenreder*

Kissing technique learned from
watching television.

—*Mark Harris*

```
Said I pulled out,
I lied.
```

—*Troy Nickerson*

**Among your sexiest
attributes: health
insurance.**

—*Jaynel Attolini*

She left all her things
behind.

—*Craig Fishburn*

Loved them all, for a
minute.

—*Ian Fischer*

Don't want your ring. Just love.

—*Naomi Piercey*

Teen homewrecker.
Still miss his kid.

—*Martha Garvey*

Hired me. Fired me.
Married me.

—*Julie Klam*

You were my Little Red-Haired Girl.

—*Patricia Bailey*

Girl beautiful. No Mercedes. No love.

—*Sujoy Kumar Chowdhury*

Jeannette's spell influences my every thought.

—*Jordan Brady*

He should have married the television.

—*Tammy Lunn*

Wined, dined, free. Bedded, wedded, flee.

—*Gail L. Jenner*

Never again. Maybe Once. Yes, okay.

—Emma Starr

He preferred buddies.
Buddy preferred me.

—Tara Lazar

Unfortunately eight
inches was not
enough.

—Steven Banks

More complicated than
movies let on.

—Erin McIntosh

Job requires me to contemplate cunnilingus.

—*Dan Savage*

I fell in love twice today.

—*Vanessa Aricco*

She got Hodgkin's lymphoma. I bailed.

—*Michael Malice*

He loved the Mac, not me . . .

—*Ellen Holmes*

Wow. Didn't think she'd do that.

—*Gary Belsky*

Maybe he will call me tomorrow.

—*Jody Madala*

Married a hottie,
divorced a hothead.

—*Pixie Paradiso*

Shhh. You won't feel a thing.

—*Emily Doherty*

Me, wife, boyfriend;
polyamory can work.

—*Amy Collins*

Bemoaning the memory of
unreciprocated affection.

—*Francis DiClemente*

I love you and I'm leaving.

—*Christine Stewart*

Said no. Twice. When is yes?

—*Lisa Brennan-Jobs*

`Went for milk,`
`never came back.`

—*Lindsay Freda*

Well, my children still love me.

—*Bill Shapiro*

We kissed before
he was arrested.

—*Melissa Jun Rowley*

Sex. Three weeks
from Thursday, OK?

—*Adam L. Penenberg*

Happiness is a bed to
myself.

—*Michelle Ponto*

I kicked Romeo's ass. The End.

—*Lee Payne*

**After a divorce,
orgasms are possible.**

—*Becky Judge*

Beloved's face.
Like staring at God.

—*Susan Dickman*

He sees the me I don't.

—*Mary Catherine Hamelin*

Concern with freedom became his
bondage.

—*Teresa Lin*

I have never been in love.

—*Peter Blue*

```
We can share secrets
and bras.
```

—*Caroline Paul*

eHarmony reject, Match.com failure,
unloveable me.

—*Tammy L. Denton*

Looked, liked, lusted, loved, lost, lonely.

—*Susan Hale*

Gone. His child grows inside me.

—*Veronica Keegan-Moore*

"I don't cheat."
"You do now."

—*Christopher Sorrentino*

Love, unreturned
is still worth
feeling.

—*Lisa Stanton*

Birthday cake one day late.
Forgiven.

—*Tricia Callahan*

It hurts even worse
in French.

—*Derek Pollard*

She married another guy.
Her loss.

—*Will Allen*

I love you but
fuck you.

—*Dean Haspiel*

86

Gave my heart;
lost a friend.

—*Johan Dahlberg*

Sixteen, forced to have
an abortion.

Lynne Bailey

Loved him.
Hated her.
Now gay.

—*Paul Wysocki*

They all came
before they left.

—*Scott O'Neil*

She looked at me and ran.

—*Matt LoGuercio*

**I am a goddess.
Please agree.**

—*Abiola Abrams*

We "I do"-ed.
Then, he didn't.

—*Lisa Parrack*

I was smitten, now I'm smote.

—*Bobby Wynne*

Much married, fourth time is charmed.

—*Erica Jong*

Saw, meet, kiss,
live, share, betray.

—*Chris Witko*

She then turned,
laughed, and left.

—*David Abutbul*

She owns my heart, always will.

—*Scott Lynn*

Was a tramp;
now a feminist.

—*Evelyn Sharenov*

My sluggish laptop;
his archived porn.

—*Lara Tupper*

Slept with most of my friends.

—*Lisa Haines*

Couldn't save him.
Thought I could.

—*Jiffy Page*

I want to flip my claddagh.

—*Joann Wang*

My marital advice?
Marry an orphan.

—*Kristina Wright*

Seventeen, already love
being the mistress.

—*Molly Savage*

Only feels right when it's not.

—*Mary Miller*

It's better when
you're the celebrity.

—*Lux Alptraum*

Our song:

Pat Benetar's

"We Belong."

—*Daniel Handler*

We touch each other, 8500km apart.

—Michelle Yoon

Zooey Glass is my
only love.

—Beth Dunigan

Dogs remain

faithful,

husband off leash.

—Gail Reilly

He picked Jets over sex. Sigh.

—Paula Edgar

Best first date ever. Then, nothing.

—Tsia Christina Harris

Love is living
on Avenue D.

—Virginia Graham

My stockings looked better on him.

—Renee Guillory

Tomorrow, maybe, I'll
sell the ring.

—Matt Tanner

My least favorite word is platonic.

—*Nicole Bohn*

```
Flicked my Bic;
busted my bubble.
```

—*Bird E. Miller*

In reunion dream,
you had hair.

—*Sarah Bird*

**My self-esteem
died that day.**

—*Sandi Brown*

I searched him on Google.
Nothing.

—*Cybele O'Brien*

He lied, I cried, love died.

—*Jeanette Cheezum*

Tired of hurting me, she said.

—*John Sheffield*

He was The One.
I wasn't.

—*Cathy Collinson*

Wonder-filled, and

98

never a dull torment.

—*Diane Ackerman*

Polaroid Love: Right
there. Click, whirrrrr.

—*Jay Randall*

Wonder Woman fell for
Green Lantern.

—*Kellie Dooher*

I love penises
more than chocolate.

—*Mary Chang*

Marriage, children, empty nest:
now what?

—*Oliver House*

Pining. Falling. Crashing.
Burning. Not interested.

—*Stephanie Gerst*

Didn't realize I'd still be lonely.

—*Pamela Cash*

He was French and I wasn't.

—*Ann Lamas*

Irish guys are easy.
Crabs suck.

—*Alexa Joy Sherman*

Will luck hold? Jury still out.

—*Darin Strauss*

Found him at Crazy Horse Saloon.

—*Stephanie Robertson*

Love makes the world go stupid.

—*David Sandler*

Longed for opportunity . . . then you knocked.

—*Katie Williams*

Kim sang, "Let's stay together."
Accomplished.

—*Patrick J. Sauer*

Plenty of liquor—
we'll make it.

—*Allison Shields*

They never seemed
crazy at first.

—*Eric Heiman*

True love is a nephew's hug.

—*Alison Schulak-Moore*

First kissed a girl at sixteen.

—*Christina Santos*

Grew up on border, loved across.

—*Erin Oldroyd*

It's lonely here on the shelf.

—*Genevieve Stanhope*

I put
the seat
down
now.

—*Marcus Eder*

He changed me. I outgrew him.

—*Marcie Vargas*

Love means lying about my
weight.

—*Ann Ingalls*

**Diagnosis: Bipolar.
He still loves me.**

—*Valerie Elliott*

Smile all day.
Cry all night.

—*Tran Le Mai*

She defines happiness.
I defy gravity.

—*Dan Rubin*

**Proposal. Dowry.
Betrothal. Marriage.
Children. Love.**

—*Mitali Perkins*

He cheated and then
he died.

—*Judy McGuire*

So this is me, getting out.

—*Stephanie Brady*

Tissues everywhere,
for semen, for tears.

—*Matt Sullivan*

I'm too old
for this shit.

—*Abby Ellin*

Three engagement rings.
No wedding band.

—*Sadie Pfannkuche*

He married someone else
named Christine.

—*Christine Stanley*

A virgin! He's infuriated;
she's devastated.

—*Kristine Eckis*

Brad Pitt missed out big time.

—*Erin Walsh*

Palindromantically:
Eros saw I was sore.

—*Aaron Fagan*

Got it right second time around.

—*Gina di Bari Carlos*

Like *Poltergeist*, without all the ghosts.

—*John Palmer Jr.*

I'm fifty-three, he's thirty-six, why not?

—*Wendy Green*

His e-mail password was the same.

—*Alexander Chee*

Now I hate hearing that song.

—*T'Anna Holst*

Happily single. No one believes me.

—Eliot Sheridan

Somehow I even love
his snoring.

—Lauren Given

Overwrought, fraught,
we fought over naught.

—Gail Siegel

Broken heart so
I tried suicide.

—Phillip Seep

Find, feel, fuck, forgive, forget. Fantastic.

—Janice Dickinson

He killed the baby I wanted.

—*LaDonna Jean Jacobsen*

No closet could
hide this
love.

—*Andrea Dela Cruz*

Divorce papers served on
first anniversary.

—*Vicki Botnick*

Knew cat would accept
you, eventually.

—*Anne Ursu*

I waited. He never
called back.

—*Amy Black*

Love has healed my
many wounds.

—*Inara de Luna*

Years of pillow talk.
BlackBerry breakup.

—*Kathryn Aronsohn*

Too optimistic for my own good.

—*Joyce Riley*

Loved him until nothing was left.

—*Jackie Hodges*

She came back,
I wasn't home.

—*Erik Raske*

Bastard turned out to be
straight.

—*Lanford Wilson*

**Jumped in young,
still going strong.**

—*Laura Scott*

Actually, I took my own
virginity.

—*Alison Carey*

Before you, love was
vainglorious chimera.

—*Loretta Serrano*

**Wife. Daughter. Dog.
Home. Miss them.**

—*Joe Doyle*

Someone should've objected at my
wedding.

—*Cynthia Ceilan*

Want to return mail-order bride.

—David Tamarin

**A short affair
but pure lust.**

—Spencer Wendt

**He would have
been my forever.**

—Tina Blanchard

Heart swells, tears
come, "I do."

—Laurie Simpkinson

How can I build trust again?

—*Neil Strauss*

My uterus hurts like my heart.

—Jennifer Coleman

Received "counseling voucher" as wedding gift.

—Jessika Blanton

Long-distance love. Short-distance lust.

—Robin Boord

Starving artist lived on love: broke.

—Kara Bernatowicz

I need a looser deadline, baby.

—Ryan Hagen

I wasn't looking.
She found me.

—Hal Isaacson

**He had nothing.
Gave me everything.**

—Rebecca Woolf

Bad idea being wife
number four.

—MJ Miller

She said she was a he.

—*Paul Morris*

Three-word memoir: Paper. Pen.
Revenge.

—*Lora Mitchell*

**Death, divorce,
heartbreak, cancer.
Chocolate helped.**

—*Linda Farbstein*

My ex ended up
on *Oprah.*

—*Michele Menzia*

Everyone's crazy except you and me.

—*Mark Frauenfelder*

Let's live on an island together.

—*Carla Sinclair*

His fists loved me. He didn't.

—*Andrea Paloian*

Bankrupt man
marries and
bankrupts me.

—*Edie More*

A threesome in
Portugal. Nothing
  happened.

—*Julia Slotnik Sturm*

She broke my heart
by e-mail.

—*Dan Rollman*

Two marriages.
  The wrong one died.

—*Anne Hamilton*

Ecstasy. Exquisite pain. What's the difference?

—*Adrian King*

Stopped wanting Mr. Perfect,
found him.

—*Bob Morris*

Couldn't count . . . on him either.

—*L. J. Williamson*

Found fellow cliff-diver. Best risk ever.

—*Piper Kerman*

Love—an invitation

to climb trees?

—*Joanne Harris*

**Second time around,
I got luckier.**

—*Joan Leibovich*

Found true love
at a funeral.

—*Ted Sutton*

Engaged in Jerusalem.
Thank you, God.

—*Lynn Harris*

The couch is actually quite
comfortable.

—*Beth Cato*

**Endurance is an
expression of love.**

—*Lee Woodruff*

**Our prison visitations
were surprisingly romantic.**

—*Larry Smith*

Wedding day:
MIL bet we'd divorce.

—*Susan Henderson*

**Sorry, it was
the Paxil
talking.**

—*Sam Seder*

Best family ever.
Thank you, Match.com!

—*Alexa Young*

I fixed him but broke myself.

—*Amal Khairul*

Girl loves, but boy loves boy.

—*Sandra Jackson*

I finally threw away his
toothbrush.

—*Rachel Fershleiser*

**He was attracted
to crippled girls.**

—*Terri Wagener*

We'll break up
before this prints.

—*Porochista Khakpour*

It's just a matter of luck.

—Ayelet Waldman

Call when you get home safely.

—Crissa-Jean Chappell

I'm your one that got away.

—Mary Elizabeth Williams

In hindsight, I'd still choose you.

—Natana Gill

It happened in a
graceless kiss.

—*Caroline Sun*

I told you it affects me.

—*Carrie Kania*

Cynical New Yorker
convinced of soulmate.

—*Kate Hamill*

Romantic comedies
screwed me for life.

—*Daniela Medina*

May
I
have
the
last
dance?

—*Robert Hass*

About the Editors

SMITH Magazine founding editor Larry Smith has worked as an editor at *Men's Journal*, *ESPN: The Magazine*, and *Might*. His writing has appeared in the *New York Times*, the *Los Angeles Times*, *Popular Science*, *Salon*, and many other places. Rachel Fershleiser is SMITH's memoir editor and has written for the *Village Voice*, *New York Press*, *Print*, and *National Post*. Larry and Rachel edited the *New York Times* bestseller *Not Quite What I Was Planning: Six-Word Memoirs by Writers Famous & Obscure*. Both live in New York City.